PARTICLES IN MOTION

AJ SAUR

murmuration
press™

Particles in Motion
Copyright © 2019 AJ Saur
All rights reserved.

Book design: Amy Cole
Cover art: Amy Cole

ISBN: 978-1-946671-11-0

Printed in the United States of America

Body text is typeset in Adobe Garamond. Headings are typeset in ABeeZee

Murmuration Press

To contact the publisher concerning this book or others like it, email: murmurationpress@gmail.com

For the unsettled
and SDG

INTRODUCTION

On our honest days, we may admit there appears no way forward in this world. The sighing distance only seems to grow like an endless exhale. How far must we go to finally breathe in?

ACKNOWLEDGEMENTS

This collection would have stalled without the faithful encouragement and editorial support of so many people. My sincerest gratitude to Jane Wheeler—everything you touch not only comes to life, it sings across the page. I also offer my appreciation to Amy Carpenter-Leugs, Jerel Domer, and Keith McAdams who provided critical feedback on the trajectory of most (if not all) of these poems. Thanks to Amy Cole of JPL Design Solutions who blew me away with her design of this book.

To my dear friends John and Hannah Marie Roberts, thank you for your loving support when I wanted to drop kick this collection across the room. To the amazing Stephen and Annie Panaggio, thank you for helping me believe I could land in the shoes of a poet one day. And to my beautiful mother, thank you for faithfully reading all of these poems even though poetry doesn't blow your hair back.

ACCOMPANIMENT

I offer my gratitude to these amazing artists who provided a musical lift to these poems: Asaf Avidan, Jeff Buckley, Tracy Chapman, Bob Dylan, Abel Korzeniowski, Alexi Murdoch, Over the Rhine, Max Richter, and the Robert Shaw Festival Singers.

TABLE OF CONTENTS

ONE

Particles in Motion 17

Fear Ye Not 18

Enemies on Every Side 20

Pegasus Descending...21

Shower 22

Untouched 23

It is hard for you to kick against the goads...24

Dreaming...25

Assimilation 27

Loneliness 28

Entropy Needs No Fuel..29

Leaving the womb may have been my first mistake 30

Open wide your mouth and I will fill it...31

Floating..32

Above the Clouds 33

Mostly Cloudy 34

On Fire 36

On Fire Too 38

An Artist in his Studio on Ash Wednesday 40

Ash Wednesday Afterlife...41

Epiphany..42

Eternal God of Contingent Things..44

Repaving Remembrance Road...45

He who has eyes, let him see..46

Upstream 48

Fishing 50

Nearsighted..52

His Eye is on the Sparrow...54

Inside Voice..55

Static...56

Solace...57

Center...59

TWO

Let There Be...63

Falling Doesn't Always Hurt...64

Desert Praise 65

A Day in the Sun...66

Dawn 68

Barber 69

The Weight 71

Holy Spirits..72

Centerpiece 74

The Woman in the Black Dress...75

Breaking Up on the Winter Solstice 76

Embodied 78

600 Thread Count Sheets...79

Habitation..80

Crocus Coup...81

The Stones Will Cry Out 82

THREE

Iconoclast...85

In the Name of the Father, the Son, and Wile E. Coyote................86

Pentecost..88

The Scar..89

After Christmas...90

Anointing..91

Thy Kingdom Come..92

Fear of the Lord..93

FOUR

The Leap Second..99
Perichoresis Seeks a Fourth 101
A Single Life..102
Born and Reborn...103

FIVE

The First Law of Love 107
The Second Law of Love 108

A poem about the entire universe

HE LOVED THEM TO THE END.

~ John 13:1

ONE

PARTICLES IN MOTION

Today I heard a scientist report
that the universe continues to expand
at an escalating pace.

Farther and faster atoms race apart
out into the darkness
eternal explorers traveling away

from that loud first gathering—
searching, seeking, yearning
for the silent edge.

But there is no last cliff
no soft valley landing
said the scientist,

this modern soothsayer sadly marveling
at the separation of all things
until they are at last nothing.

I wonder if, after the interview,
he turned his car toward home and accelerated
with the solitary mission

of embracing his children
before they drift off to sleep
and forever out of his   reach.

FEAR YE NOT

They didn't understand it then
straining against the oars
backs curved like the
question marks in their minds.

For when the wind picked up
conversation died down
leaving anxious tongues to drift
over salty lips unquenched.

Exhausted eyes searched
for a light, a horizon, a hope.
Instead, what they saw out there
in the chop of those black waves

only increased their fear—
a phantom, an apparition
foretelling their demise.
But no, wait!

It's a man, *their man*
with wet feet
and a fixed gaze—
a walking lighthouse.

Only later did they comprehend
his words that night
brought to the surface
by another violent wind

pressing hard against them
this time on dry land
with tongues of fire
licking their lips.

Now they stand straight-spined
open wide their arms like sails
allow this new wind to take them out
into darkness, into lands not their own.

I hate you, I hate you, I hate you,

she says with her tight, trill voice—
rapid fire rancor from her hideout high
in the hickory tree.

I hate you, I hate you, I hate you.

I can't see her from where I stand,
but I imagine her there spying me
down the scope of her beak
lining up the shot with her small, round eyes.

I hate you, I hate you, I hate you.

Eyes as dark as the clouds that have now
maneuvered into position overhead
heavy with their artillery of rain
that soon begins rat-tat-tatting me
with a barrage of

I hate you, I hate you, I hate you.

Even as the clouds fly off, frogs emerge
from the mud and wait for me to pass by—
ground detonations set to explode
with their low, booming

I hate you, I hate you, I hate you.

When did nature become so cruel, I wondered
as I ran away in retreat,
my heart beating fiercely in my chest.

PEGASUS DESCENDING

As a child I envisioned him emerging
from a grove of clouds
at a full-winged gallop
shod with lightning
bolting through a field of blue.

Sometimes Bellerophon would be perched
on his back peering over a wing
with wonder. Other times he descended
from Olympus guided only by an invisible
muse, his reins of rhyme streaming behind—
long lines in the sky grabbed by every poet dreaming.

Today, though, he travels by FedEx.
Loaded into the belly of a Boeing,
he enjoys all-you-can-eat alfalfa, buckets of Evian,
and in-air grooming. Children no longer look up
to trail his path across the heavens for he, like they,
is only interested in a destination.

And so he will arrive
after a short thirty-minute flight
mountaintop views distant
out the window, wings folded
comfortably at his sides.

SHOWER

You enter naked, stripped
of those last vestiges of vanity.
Everything's now out in the open.
This is finally the you *you* are.

And you are welcome here
with a warm caress poured
gentle over bent head,
burdened shoulders.

Close your eyes
give yourself to it,
let its love roll down,
touch every imperfect thing

even the in-between places,
those cracks that won't close.
Stand here. Don't move.
Don't consider your way forward—

the endless attire of a clothed world.
Steep in this moment
become rich, full-bodied.
Then worship.

Sing your off-key song of thanksgiving.
Hear your voice returned different,
more true. Yes, the world will
ravage you, but don't despair.

You can come back tomorrow
renew your friendship with tile
and faucet, with that admiring drain
always looking up to you.

UNTOUCHED

I wake from dagger dreams
searching for a victim
and all too gladly play the part

Exploring my frame's weakness
I find the spot soft
warm beneath my fingers

slide the blade in
between ribs seeking
my caged enemy

But the steel
too short
emerges with nothing

Pulling back the flesh
I see him there beating
his defiant rhythm

But no matter how I tilt
or shake myself
I can't quite grasp him—

a coward
evading
the fight

IT IS HARD FOR YOU TO KICK AGAINST THE GOADS

True.
But I do it anyway
and will keep at it.

You'll ask why,
of course.
I'll respond

the only way I know
by lowering my head
and kicking.

You'll inquire if it hurts.
My spilt blood
will answer.

You may sigh.
Shake your head.
Perhaps even love me

with your eyes.
I will look ahead.
Plod on.

Keep wondering
when death
becomes life.

DREAMING

I awoke in a body.
Different than the one
I inhabited moments before.

One in which I held
a small dog, stroked her head,
but didn't hatch an evil plot.

No, I sat outside a café in Paris,
sun warming my face,
a book open on the table.

I stopped reading to consider
the dog at my fingertips, where she was
as she slept on my lap—

perhaps in the body of a Great Dane
traipsing through a stream, trailing
a squirrel through a strand of poplar trees.

Or maybe she became human
to search me out, to inform me
the generic dog food has to go.

Wherever she was,
her wagging tail suggested
considerable action was afoot.

Much more action
than can be said of this body
in which I now awake.

I could not say who inhabited it
before I got here and why
it was left in such a state.

Don't get me wrong,
I am happy to share.
I only wish whoever it was

had the courtesy to get up
and brew a fresh pot of coffee
before I arrived.

ASSIMILATION

On Saturday mornings
the runners arrive in waves
at my local coffee shop
in their fluorescent shirts
and expensive shoes
coasting to the counter
from 5 or 10 kilometers away.

Today, they appeared in pairs
much the same way those young men
from The Church of Latter-day Saints
landed on my doorstep last evening.
How bright these men looked
in their white starched shirts
their faces beaming
with belief in the unbelievable.

They gave off the same glow
found in the eyes of the women who
once flowed into my father's boutique,
their floral print dresses
billowing in their wake,
their tall hats like flags
declaring allegiance to high fashion.

Even they,
liberated women,
couldn't escape the rudder
of replication steering them
into a dense fog,
a Bermuda Triangle of being
where all are lost.

LONELINESS

Scientists say our neurons can snap
fifty times per second.
I guess I shouldn't be surprised
that I can't keep up with myself.

So much information passes
just below the skin, my body
sharing secrets I can't comprehend.
Perhaps my gurgling stomach,

that insistent pulse at my wrist
are trying to tell me
how much I am loved,
but I may never know.

Yet, I will continue to feed myself
wear sweaters to keep warm
in hopes that one day
those things spoken in the dark

may be grasped in the light,
that one day
I will catch up with myself
or be caught.

ENTROPY NEEDS NO FUEL

That new car smell always fades
exits through the powered windows
past the perfectly positioned windshield
out over the sparkling hood

which you wish would blind you,
pull a hood over your head
so you can't see everything go
downhill.

Even Moses had his veil
and you need something
to keep yourself from yourself
and the traffic jam of thoughts

lining up, reminding you
that no one gets out of this alive,
no thing is the one thing
you can ride forever.

But you've got these wheels
and they're still moving.
So crank up those tunes,
drive hard down the hill.

Who knows, you may just catch
the shimmer of his spoiler
taking the next curve, reflecting
those last beams of the fading sun.

LEAVING THE WOMB MAY HAVE BEEN MY FIRST MISTAKE

I throw wide my limbs
in the late summer sun
grabbing at every last inch of warmth
before the cold sets in.

For this effort, add my name
to that list of explorers who set out
in search of a new land,
an open country

where they could plant a flag,
stake a claim.
Like tongues of flame
testing the wild edges

we reach out   and out   and out.
But will the surrounding darkness
of the deep sea floor
or those furthest stretches

of space keep us warm,
keep that little light of our souls lit?
Perhaps we've gotten it all wrong
heading out instead of in.

Maybe it's only when we're suspended,
going nowhere, that we find ourselves
at home—fed and warmed by another
with nothing to do but be.

OPEN WIDE YOUR MOUTH AND I WILL FILL IT

We all start connected,
tethered to a source through
which every desire is met.

There is no rumbling stomach,
no need to lift a heavy fork
to one's mouth.

There are no lonely nights,
no feet left cold.
The world is everything it should be

and we don't fear the dark.
We are content
to let the future remain the future—

that cascade of days
buffered by a belly.
But, one day, we're severed

from the stalk
arranged neatly in a crib
like a fresh bouquet.

We always remember, though,
that time before dawn
when we were attached to another and full.

If we're honest, every day
we try to find our way back there.
Someday, I suspect, we'll make it.

FLOATING

I drift on my back
    unmoored
from the shore of this lake

watching clouds
    caravan
through a small slice of sky

I hear the wind
    whisper
through distant reeds

relaying fluid
    secrets
I cannot hear

My limbs are
    loosed
from gravity's grip

and my mind is
    adrift
in the ever expanding

                universe

ABOVE THE CLOUDS

It used to be quiet here,
a place where a god could think—
plenty of open space and clear airwaves.

But now the traffic is tyrannical.
A herd of jets stampeding
across the white plains without pause,

without progression, endless loops
to the same destination. Much like
their passengers crisscrossing the heavens

advancing, retreating, searching for home—
thousands of anxious minds grinding away
louder than any plane,

breaking the sound barrier,
splitting the sacred shell of every edge
of this once silent frontier.

Even the distant moon
can't escape the clamor—
the bounding footfalls, the crack

of a golf ball.
The poor stars have no idea
what's about to hit them.

When the cloud descended
filling the temple
was it of the cumulus variety

with its fluffy whiteness snuggling
the freshly hewn stone, cuddling
the newly carved cherubim?

Was it so thick the priests floated out
through the decorative doors
like Aladdin on a wool carpet?

This is how my Sunday School teacher
described the scene as she moved
the great cloud across the flannelgraph board

letting her hand linger
on the plush white cutout.
Never mind that her cloud

looked like a giant piece of popcorn
similar to what we'd receive
that morning for a snack.

What six year-old wouldn't want a God
who fills his temple floor-to-ceiling
with appropriately seasoned goodness?

And how pleased our parents were
when we showed them
our cotton ball cloud craft

and proclaimed our love for
this Orville Redenbacher
redeemer.

Only later did we discover
the Sinai-cloud God,
gray and mysterious.

Only after we invited him,
sharp with lightning,
to dwell within.

ON FIRE

Push back the furniture
Clear a space in the sanctuary

Lay me out straight
a faggot for Christ

Walk around me seven times
Offer your silent prayers

Beat your breast
if necessary

Then wait
It will happen

or it won't

Pillar or tongue
or live coal from the altar

Or nothing

The Spirit proceeds
unpredictably

Of course
there's always self-immolation

but that's a momentary light
Make me a boundless blaze

or back away

I'm dry wood
will spark at your touch—

a pyre
fit for a thousand sacrifices

maybe more

ON FIRE TOO

You're a pyre
awaiting a spark

Strike up
the praise band

sing the songs
with real gusto

your flame
is almost lit

Don't worry
if nothing comes down

from above,
that pillar

of paternal
pyrotechnics

for feelings
can combust

make fine tinder
for self-immolation

So stand up
raise your hands

spread your mass—
you're about to become

a glow stick
for God

a mesmerizing
gleam

to your neighbors

AN ARTIST IN HIS STUDIO ON ASH WEDNESDAY

It begins with fire
white heat blazing
a trail black—a way
to follow

And he does
ambles through ashes
finds the burning
turn within

So he prepares his paint—
a small bowl of darkness
collected from the soles
of his shoes

The canvases file into his studio
some fresh, newly stretched
others worn by weather
and wrinkled

He doesn't use brush
trowel or knife
prefers the feel
of pigment on fingertips

as he labors over each piece—
adds his mark
whispering a prayer
that they go forth

ablaze

ASH WEDNESDAY AFTERLIFE

I bow my head
over the sink
where water plays
on my fingers

a cascading closing hymn
echoing off ceramic tile
joining the unending song
of the seraphim

I turn the faucet, raise
the sound of their voices
catch the warm chorus
in my cupped hands

then baptize myself—
tear the temporal
Past, Present, Future
meet at the crossroad

of my forehead
then depart as friends
follow the furrowed lines
of my face, carry me

down death's drain
When the final gurgle
is gone from the pipes
I open my eyes to discover

a blank mirrored
reflection
and a dusty residue
rimming the bowl

EPIPHANY

Glory always fades,
just ask Moses about
the bag over his head.

Or inquire with anyone
whose fifteen minutes
have come and gone.

A star may rise in the east,
but sooner or later
it will set in the west.

It's been said
that famous people
die in threes; perhaps

this collective dimming
eases us more gently
into the night.

The Magi also traveled as a trio,
played their gig in Bethlehem
then dissolved

into the pages of history.
But they didn't return
the same way they came.

Maybe that's true of us all
as we journey from
darkness to darkness.

We find a different way home
or a new home all together—
one beyond the horizon,

beyond this business of
day and night,
rising and setting.

ETERNAL GOD OF CONTINGENT THINGS

I awaken after midnight
to winter's wolves howling
outside my window. As I pull
the blanket up under my chin

I can't help but wonder
if a howl is still a howl
if no one like me is startled
out of sleep to hear it.

Of course, this remains
the age-old question
whether falling trees, like toddlers,
swallow their cries

if no one is present
with an attentive ear,
a caring embrace.
For what's a noise

if its waves never break
on someone's shore?
We live in a world afloat
with ears and eyes and hands

looking for an outlet, a connection
hot with electricity.
And when we find one
we hold on tight

as this merry-go-round world
spins about a sun which,
now hidden in the night,
will soon illumine this room.

REPAVING REMEMBRANCE ROAD

They begin work before the sun
throws off the covers of the horizon
and heaves herself up in search
of a strong cup of coffee.

They too have their minds
on a warm brew as they zip up
their bright yellow vests becoming
a constellation of stars

circling the construction site,
radiating heat as they jack-hammer
then claw away layer after layer
of worn and weary pavement.

Midday, they stop
to wipe the glistening
beads from their foreheads,
to marvel at the core of brick

exposed at their feet.
Their silence is quickly broken
by beeping backhoes retreating
with years in their buckets.

There is no time to wonder
about the people
who once walked here.
They must move on.

The sun alone
now high in the sky
looks far away and distant
lost in her memories.

HE WHO HAS EYES, LET HIM SEE

The peaks of my hair
have turned white

skin's smooth places
now rough

a new mountain rises
in my gut

I will miss
those first lands

so level and sure
underfoot

But terrains
have shifted

and I can no longer lift
myself

to view
the stunning vistas

So I must learn
to walk again

a seeing by touch,
by feeling

in the growing darkness
It's tempting

to stay
down

to resolve
to move no further

for every territory
has its terror

and wonder
for those who rise up

to behold it

UPSTREAM

I am not this stream
bending gently around
a strand of trees, a path

of least resistance.
I could be
if I believed

the end
is a soft drop
into the waiting hands

of a placid lake,
a calm sea.
But who knows

if this way becomes a torrent,
a racing to the edge
of a steep waterfall,

a mighty crashing down.
Or, perhaps worse,
a drifting away

until everything dries up,
a cracked river bed,
a lonely last resting place.

So, I will not go easily
get swept away.
I'll make demands.

Be willful.
Carve my own path
through the hard rock.

And you will let me
until I'm crushed or
drowned in my own desires

then you'll say again
This way
and I might follow.

FISHING

Every Sunday morning
a faithful few men
gather on the bridge
when traffic is thin

and you can hear the line unspool
from the reel
like a windup toy let loose
with its merry whir.

Even as their wives assemble
for the 7 a.m. Mass
lighting candles and casting
prayers heavenward,

they light cheap cigars
and fling
hope
into the abyss.

Most manage several poles
harnessing them to the rail
with a bungee or bit of rope.
Occasionally

a man will rise
from his lawn chair
to refill a foam cup
with coffee from a thermos.

Most just sit, look out
periodically tilt a head back
to exhale puffs of smoke
into the brightening sky

where the sun, now unhooked
from the horizon, casts its light
causing the lines to sparkle
like a brilliant revelation.

NEARSIGHTED

I marvel that my genes,
worn and faded,
continue to be handed down

father to daughter,
mother to son
each successive generation

further from the original—
crisp seams, clearly defined
curves of the double-helix.

Apparently my ancestors
were farsighted enough
to slip a folded bill into

Mother Nature's bloomers,
a tip for the slight tipping
of the scale in our direction.

What could be more natural
than to select yourself in, especially
when you can scarcely see the scale

let alone forage for food,
arrow an elk, start a fire
to warm your genome by?

Or perhaps luck left them large signs—
visions to show them the way.
Or maybe a clear-sighted muse

deposited morsels directly
into their mouths
determined to preserve

our perspective of the world—
our golden halos encircling
even the dimmest light,

our indiscriminate
washes of color
the greens the blues the reds

running into each other
a blur of difference
getting along just fine.

HIS EYE IS ON THE SPARROW

I felt sad for the starling
splitting her seed several
feet from where she stalled
my morning walk.

Eyeing me, she tilted
her head sideways
as if to say, *At least I'm a bird*
and not this seed.

"A strong argument,"
I admitted aloud, my voice
startling her to flight.
I wish I could fly off with her

see everything from above:
the silver shimmer of minnows
dancing in the heart of a stream;
the field of corn, its twirling tassels

cheering every passing cloud;
the group of golden-haired girls
chalking the sidewalk
with sunny messages for strangers.

But even these seem
just the tip of things—
the visible point
of a whole hidden world

discovered only when all senses
are senseless
and that still small soul
becomes guide.

INSIDE VOICE

How loud it is in my head
with its incessant thumping
on my inner ear, playing a tune
to which it expects me to march.

This is no little drummer boy song
soft and slow
but a full percussion ensemble
continually banging.

When the brass section trumpets in
from another lobe, I know
it will keep me awake tonight
with its concert of endless notes—

bad jazz at a dry club, me dying
for a drink.
Much the same way
the woman at the next table

appears in need
of a stiff mid-day cocktail
as she again implores her child
to use his inside voice.

A request,
it seems to me,
he's heeding
with utmost obedience.

STATIC

In the slim hours of night
if I set the dial just so
I can hear her voice
her slight British accent hovering

between the hash marks
telling me how the bar-headed goose
migrates over the Himalayas
at astonishing altitudes.

How, by surfing a thermal
it moves up and down
up and down
riding the mountains' contours.

She's now whispering the story to me
and my heart beats faster
but I can't ascend high enough.
She's vanishing in the thin air.

Exhausted, I fall asleep.
I awake to discover her disappearance
behind a line of heavy snow
and imagine her there

on the other side
nestled into bed
tuning her dial
hoping to hear my voice.

SOLACE
   -After Pi Benio

Everyone hangs
by the thinnest
thread

the narrowest
branch
of an inverted tree—

roots loose
in the black soil
of space

There is nothing below us

but the expanse
of possibility

the prospect
of despair

We long
to let ourselves go

            let the wind take us

dance despite
the dangling

Still,
our bodies

are never fully
our own

never free of past
choices

or fated
occurrences

Yet, we do move
        for a moment

alive
in an old course

new to us
        a swaying in time

Our neighbors
too

tremble
        in their own way

our bodies
        briefly touching

CENTER

You are the temple of God
and the Spirit of God
dwells in you? ~ 1 Cor. 3:16

My eyes are stained glass windows
femurs ivory columns, my ribs
rows of pews for the faithful

undulating with each breath
carried out into the world by a wind
that's always been blowing

I too am on the move
a building on the go
make wide arcs around town

circle something unseen
the way the sun orbits a bigger body,
a greater force

Straight lines
do not exist in nature
everything bends, turns

in its own way
We must learn to ride the edges
find them narrow, a funnel

to the center—
an altar,
a heart

TWO

LET THERE BE

In the beginning
God hovered,
a mother
drawing up
a chair beside

hand gentle on
round belly
chin resting on
the cool wood
of a crib

There, she speaks
quietly down
into a space
that soon will nestle
an untamable light

There, her mouth
sends forth waves
bearing dreams
and visions, hopes
and fears

a full heart set sail
toward a distant
harbor, toward
an end
with no ending

FALLING DOESN'T ALWAYS HURT

It's when the sugar maples lining
our driveway turn the color of your hair
that my thoughts most often turn to you.

To the way the orange curls lining
your face tumbled toward earth
when you bent to pick up

a perfect leaf to press
between the pages of your Bible.
I never told you I collected

a strand of it a few weeks
before it fell out
without changing color—

a piece of gold I buried
in a book of love poems.
Every autumn I unearth it,

press it between my palms
and marvel that its color remains
as vibrant as the sunlight

that streamed into our room
on the quiet morning when
a last breath fell from your lips.

DESERT PRAISE

After the storm

the silence
the lightening sky
the rippling air

steam rising
like a multitude
of uplifted hands

A DAY IN THE SUN

I raked the sun today
until my hands blistered
but my heart didn't melt
not even when I harvested

armfuls of light
clutching it tightly to my chest
before plunging it into
the darkness

of a yard waste bag.
After a few hours
I had blotted out
the entire solar surface

lining up the last of it
on the curb
next to a broken chair
the garbage man refuses to pick up.

But he will haul away the sun
heave bag after bag
into his truck
where every bit of gold

will be tarnished
by banana peels and sad flowers
that once looked so bright
next to someone's bed.

A thought
which so stirs my heart
that I heave up
from my recliner

lumber down the driveway
and pour out
a single bag—gilt adorning
a green canvas.

Turning away, I raise
my face
to the empty sky
and let myself fall

into an amber embrace.

DAWN

There was a time
we rose to the rhythm
of her unhurried breath
our souls slowly lifted
from an ocean of sleep, drawn
through shallow waters
to the shore of day.

But times have changed.

We have exchanged
her seasoned skills
with the sharp sound
of an alarm clock
its insistent beeping
a drumbeat of life
unto death.

All the while she waits

until we grow old, tired
until we can no longer
keep the cadence.
Then she will come again
do her slow work
release us lightly
onto the sands

of a new day.

BARBER

Our bodies are the earth we carry. ~ Augustine

He plays in the dirt all day
running his hands through
thick black soil, sandy soil,

soil as white as the beaches of Waikiki
collecting samples on his sleeves
helping bear our load for a spell.

It feels like magic, or a miracle
the way his meticulous cuts
free us from the weight of our lives.

He works with such care
brushing bits of us
from our burdened necks

gently uncovering our ears
so we can hear him marvel
at the coming of spring, the possibility

of the Cubs winning it all—
releasing us
from a different weight.

He always ends by applying
a warm towel to our heavy eyes
relieving them

for a moment
of their labor, their straining to steer
our world toward a good end.

When we rise up, lighter
we don't hesitate to shake his hand,
to hold it briefly in our own,

a small token
of gratitude for his efforts
for the dirt he'll carry home tonight

under his fingernails.

THE WEIGHT

Death is heavy.
It takes six
able-bodied men
to carry it.

Even then,
they must use
a wheeled cart
to load it into
the waiting car.

Slowly,
it will move ahead
never out of sight
as they follow
one by one
to the graveyard.

HOLY SPIRITS

I have holes
I'm leaking bits
of me everywhere

It's surprising
anything's left
I mind

the gaps
seek
stoppers

What I wouldn't give
for a cement mixer
and trowel

But even cement
cracks
What then?

Perhaps I can
find one hole
to love

Praise it
for the way
it lets light in

how it bravely
opens
each day

to a world
of foreign
objects

Put aside
my contempt
for its hunger

its unending
desire
for fullness

Accept it
as kindred spirit
one that can't

keep it
together
continually travels

on empty

CENTERPIECE

Most days I go along just fine
the kids get picked up, dinner made,
laundry laundered.

Sometimes, though, something unnamed
gnaws on me, often at the borders of me
like a beetle nibbling the corner of a leaf.

Occasionally it gets a hold of the center—
that hidden core self, soft and seed-bearing.
There it chews and chews and chews

leaves an empty pod, a black hole middle.
Not the gentle glow of the moon
or even a ray of summer sun light

can pierce that darkness. On those days
the only thing that can fill my empty vase
is for someone else to be inside

like a bouquet of wildflowers
pushing flush against my edges
with color and life.

THE WOMAN IN THE BLACK DRESS

The way she sipped her cocktail,
a sunny blend of fruit swimming
in a generous sea of Seagram's,
told me everything.

The playfulness of her tongue edging
the clear plastic straw
suggested she'd tease the drink
well after sunset

in the same way
she'd tease my heart
as I walked her home that night.
And I let her

because the yellow in her glass
was like a bouquet of daffodils
lighting up her face, like fireworks
bright against the dark backdrop

of her sleeveless dress.
That there would be no fireworks
between us I knew
for she'd only allow the smallest taste

of the beverage to reach her lips
fearful of its effect on her wits
or maybe her insatiable desire
for more.

The same fear that kept her from drinking
me to the dregs, leaving only a faint
sweetness in my mouth as she faded
behind her front door.

BREAKING UP ON THE WINTER SOLSTICE

I will lie down
here

alone

between the lines
of this page, this field

of freshly fallen
snow.

I will lob snowballs,
a steady supply of cold

hard remarks
scattering everyone.

I will form a fort
adding comment

upon frozen
comment

until I'm a solid
unmovable mass.

I will try to stir
my arms and legs

create an angel
with my words—

a better version
of me.

Mostly
I will howl

into the wind
hope my hot breath

can melt
a space

big enough for us
to be.

EMBODIED

We chatted for a spell
me on this bench
you on that power line

You told me wind is a caress
a light finger across skin
a goose bump chill of being

that it recognizes our form
even when we feel lost
and shapeless—

circles our circumference
measures our mass
discovers the weight of our lives

And satisfied speaks
through a surrounding embrace
You are enough

To prove yourself true
you flew away
hugged by a breeze

leaving only a shaking
power line
and my solid self

600 THREAD COUNT SHEETS

When I finally return to you
having scaled the mountain of the day
you enfold my timbering frame
like six-hundred pairs of soft hands.

With your tiny twill thumbs
you press into tight muscles
tenderly teasing out their secrets—
those silent screams carried the day long

now gently carried out to sea
by a current of cotton. Through the night
we whisper in wordless threads—
our bodies intertwined.

When I finally drift off to sleep,
my hand on your neck,
you stay awake listening
to my breath deepen.

In the morning, all you ask is that I take you
for a spin and then let you hang out
in the warmth of the spreading sun,
the wind rustling through your fine hair.

HABITATION

The way the monarch butterfly
moves face forward
through the world
is a small miracle—

how she skips on air
generous with herself
giving first to the leaf
then the flower.

She transforms me
from caterpillar
into one who flies
arms open, eyes wide

a child marveling at creation—
the smoothness of an acorn
the cloud carnival
overhead.

I wish I was milkweed
so she would dance
on my limbs
touch me with her tongue

carry me
quietly off
to that branch
she calls home.

CROCUS COUP

They rise up in April
purple veined with white
as if stained by snow—
winter's scar
on the fresh skin of spring.

Seemingly fragile, frail
they prove surprisingly sturdy
bearing the heavy hopes
of every soul who stops to marvel,
mouth agape.

Covert color charging through
the ground's frozen front
waving their violet victory flag—
the banner under which
we huddle for a spell

long enough to shed our coats
piling them on the pavement—
a pillar of promise,
a marker
of revolution.

THE STONES WILL CRY OUT

If it was the unfolding tongue
of a tiger lily or the loosed
vocal cords of the chrysanthemum

I would expect to hear a female voice
perfuming the air with praise
to the passing prince.

But a stone shouting
always sounds male to me—
a gravely *Glory to God in the Highest*.

I could perhaps imagine
a pebble praising
with a pre-pubescent pip

or even a smooth skipping stone
singing *Hosanna* as she tiptoes
across the Jordan River.

A solid rock, though, speaks
with the voice of Dylan.
Not the young troubadour,
electric and rolling

but the Dylan of today
all marble-mouthed
magnifying the Messiah.

It would be a garbled *Glory!*
to be sure, but the harmonica solo
would cause even the angels
to pause and listen.

THREE

ICONOCLAST

I have a name I don't know.
It's carved on a stone I've never seen.
A stone that's out there somewhere

perhaps at the edge of a lake
perhaps within reach of a child
who will stuff it in his pocket,

rest it on his nightstand.
Or it will be such a smooth stone
that he'll skip it across the water

my name ringing out, echoed back
by the trees, carried off
in the throat of a sparrow

that now sits
on my windowsill singing—
the swelling of whose song

suggests the person I'm becoming
won't easily fit
on the side of a stone.

IN THE NAME OF THE FATHER, THE SON, AND WILE E. COYOTE

I don't recall
when you assigned me
the role of the Son

but I do remember
when you sent the Spirit
from on high—

our kid sister's Barbie
dive-bombing me
during our Sunday bath.

Wingless and without
proclamation, this "dove"
attacked more than alighted

upon my head.
This was after
you baptized me

in your name
and the names of a whole cast
of Looney Tunes characters.

As I went under
again and again
I couldn't help

but wonder when Jesus
first discovered
he could walk on water.

Was he as young as me
sneaking off
to race a few ducks

on some sea somewhere?
I bet he always let them win,
much like he would later

let everyone
everywhere
win.

PENTECOST

It began with a word
spoken then written
finally seared into flesh.

A word like the wind
weaving between us
between everything

where beginning is end
end a beginning
and we, one mess

of mixed material,
miraculously maintain heat.
This mystery, this puzzle

of the Pneuma seeks
neither solving nor
secure mounting

on a block of wood—
an icon for a fixed gaze.
It lives

in the wrapping of your arms
around my shoulders,
my warm breath

on your neck,
your heart pounding
in my chest.

THE SCAR

The sky wears heavy sackcloth,
covers its head with ashen clouds.
Soon it will rend its garments,
cast them down in sharp peels, tear
asunder all those gathered on the hill.

Save one. One who will instead be pierced,
opened like a dammed river—a wild course
of blood and bile that few will follow
for who can say where it leads or ends.
Better, it seems, to take up sewing

master a stitch to suture the slit
and seek a more sensible route—
a way above the clouds where the sun
always shines by day, the moon by night,
and the stars never once mention the scar.

AFTER CHRISTMAS

It lies not where it first fell.
Someone placed it here at roadside,
added a toe tag for pickup.

Its boughs now heavy with snow
still sparkle as they once did
in the bay window of this home.

And the needles, yet green,
have life to give—a gift of color
to stark souls drifting by.

How prone we are to keep our heads
down, to miss things that no longer stand,
no longer have stars in their eyes.

Those brave enough to look
might just discover holy ground
at the curb, might catch a glimpse

of the garbage man—that chariot driver
carrying so many Elijahs
to heaven.

ANOINTING

It's an unconscious habit,
the biting the edge of the lip,
the tip of the tongue appearing
at the corner of the mouth.

She would raise an index finger
and delicately slide wayward hair
behind her ears—first left then right—
as she colored the world in indigo.

So it was when she counted out
300 denarii—a year's worth of purple
for a pound of passion.
With her hair in its proper place

she could see everything:
Pharisaical jealousy, Roman fear,
death, the grave. All tucked
neatly away

out of sight.
And there it would have stayed
like that pound of nard now hidden
on the top shelf of the pantry. But

Jesus wept

and before she knew it
her hair had fallen off her ears
poured out across his worn feet
and the entire house carried the scent

of her love.

THY KINGDOM COME

Out here in the barren
lowlands I dream of hills
echoing back my name

Even the smallest incline will do
if I prostrate before it
offer my words—

      a whispered prayer in the dirt

Such a posture has a prophet made
the wilderness resounding
with the voice of God

In this wasteland
of worn hands and hearts
cracked and creviced by the sun

      everything begins anew

Reduced by heat and time
we are deserts
of concentrated hope awaiting

spring rains
which bring forth primroses—
a gleaming white bursting

      from the broken soil

FEAR OF THE LORD

Why is it
that when you say
you love me

I expect
the other shoe
to fall

and hit me square
between
my upturned eyes?

When you utter it
I tend to bite
my nails

not nervously
but to have my hand
at the ready

to fend off
falling
footwear.

Of course,
a hand
in my mouth

allows you to finally
get a word in
edgewise.

And no wonder
you want me to shut up
for I've been shutting

down for years
circling the dying
carcass of myself

like blood
circulating
through my body

looking
for some damn
way out of this closed system.

Around
and around
I go

trying every door
pursuing every passageway
hearing only the echo

of my own voice—
the resounding sound
of my own ceaseless

song
every lyric known
every chord driving me

to that same
lonely
look out.

Yet, what's out there
may be a descending
deity

determined
to kick me in the head
until I drop

my hand
and widen my lips
to receive

a body broke
open for love
of me.

FOUR

THE LEAP SECOND

It's hard to begrudge time a raise
after all she's done—
those sleepless nights
watching over a sick child,

a gentle hand
on a warm forehead;
that unending race
around the face of a clock

lap after lap
with no one offering
a cool glass of water,
a shout of encouragement.

It seems a thankless job,
everyone grabbing at you—
pushing and pulling,
wanting more of you

on a Sunday night,
less on a Friday afternoon; more
when winding through the woods
hand-in-hand with a lover,

less when that lover leaves.
So, by all means
give her an extra second
to pause in the moonlight,

to rest on a bench.
Hell, give her two seconds
to spend on herself
replaying a memory from her youth,

a note from a favorite melody,
a word that stops time

breathless.

PERICHORESIS SEEKS A FOURTH

It takes two to tango, they say.
We're odd, though
having always danced in trios.

Four, however, seems about
the right amount of company—
the perfect crowd to crowd upon

the dance floor and move, swaying
hips hugging the corner outcasts,
low dips lifting up the downtrodden.

Of course, this party got started
long ago with just three of us moving
slow, deliberate—the generous arcs

of our arms sweeping stars into place,
our perfectly positioned feet creating
verdant valleys in the new soil.

Every dance proved a success
because of our heaving breath—
the rhythmic in-and-out, our throbbing

desire for life. And a fourth was born
in our movements. We taught her
our steps, but she's more interested

in a solo career.

We hope she'll come around,
rejoin the party,
dance with us
well past dawn.

A SINGLE LIFE

The three acts concluded
The two dates marked
The one body at rest

No tiny flag flying at the finish
No wreath of flowers encircling
No crisp shots ringing out

A flock of geese flies overhead, distant
A cooling sun passes by, disinterested
A church bell rings, dissonant

    If another solitary soul stops to imagine me
    If she stands nearby, enduring the empty sky
    If she hears my voice in these rustling leaves

        Will I continue?

BORN AND REBORN

There is no easy way out of this
no easy way in

just a foreign hand pulling
into the light air

a cry of breath
a longing

to return
to swim again

in another being
to fall back

be
caught

FIVE

THE FIRST LAW OF LOVE

Who's to say how long
black holes court after
catching each other's eye,
how much dark distance
they must cover for that first kiss.

We too feel the tug
of their togetherness,
find ourselves stretched
longing to understand
the mating dance of matter—

why my center shifts
when you come near;
how your mass masters me
moving my body toward you;
how this power bends

orbits, the course
of galaxies, even
the mighty
human
heart.

THE SECOND LAW OF LOVE

Everything is one.
No matter how fast
we run, how much space
we put between
ourselves, we feel the pull.
There's a fierce force
in the universe
determined to deter
our forward progress,
our fixation with the edge.
It knows the center holds
more promise—though
the sun's core burns hottest,
though, the human heart beats
we must embrace
its heat. For this law
requires sacrifice, only
then will we ignite,
meld.

A POEM ABOUT THE ENTIRE UNIVERSE

YHWH

www.ingramcontent.com/pod-product-compliance
Lightning Source LLC
La Vergne TN
LVHW041200080426
835511LV00006B/681